## Early
# TRANSPORTATION
### Encyclopedias

# CARS

by Corey Anderson

**Early Encyclopedias**

An Imprint of Abdo Reference
abdobooks.com

**abdobooks.com**

Published by Abdo Reference, a division of ABDO, PO Box 398166, Minneapolis, Minnesota 55439.
Copyright © 2024 by Abdo Consulting Group, Inc. International copyrights reserved in all countries.
No part of this book may be reproduced in any form without written permission from the
publisher. Early Encyclopedias™ is a trademark and logo of Abdo Reference.
Printed In China
102023
012024

THIS BOOK CONTAINS
RECYCLED MATERIALS

Editor: Carrie Hasler
Series Designer: Candice Keimig

Library of Congress Control Number: 2023939672

Publisher's Cataloging-in-Publication Data

Names: Anderson, Corey, author.
Title: Cars / by Corey Anderson
Description: Minneapolis, Minnesota : Abdo Reference, 2024 | Series: Early transportation
    encyclopedias | Includes online resources and index.
Identifiers: ISBN 9781098292911 (lib. bdg.) | ISBN 9798384910855 (ebook)
Subjects: LCSH: Cars (Automobiles)--Juvenile literature. | Automobiles--Juvenile literature. |
    Automobiles--History--Juvenile literature. | Vehicles--Juvenile literature. | Transportation--
    Juvenile literature. | Encyclopedias and dictionaries--Juvenile literature.
Classification: DDC 629.224--dc23

# CONTENTS

## Let's Hit the Road!

They zoom down the street. They take us where we want to go. What are they? Cars! Cars allow people to travel, move around town, and live in new places.

Before cars, people traveled on trains or boats to get to faraway places. To travel shorter distances, people used horses and buggies. But buggies are slow. People wanted to find a way to go farther and faster. When cars were invented, people called them horseless buggies. Cars have changed a lot over time. Today, there are all kinds of cars. There is so much to discover!

**FUN FACT!**

There are more than 1 billion cars on Earth!

## How a Gas-Powered Car Works

First, a mix of gas and air enters the engine. It makes small explosions. The explosions push the pistons. The pistons move up and down.

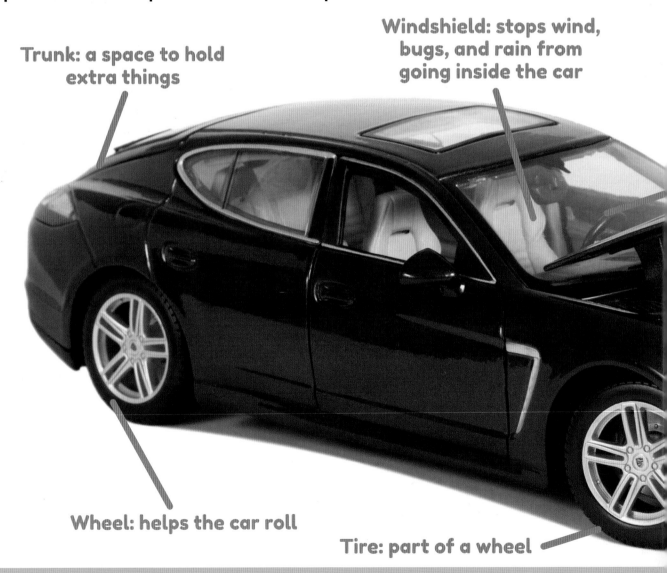

Trunk: a space to hold extra things

Windshield: stops wind, bugs, and rain from going inside the car

Wheel: helps the car roll

Tire: part of a wheel

The engine powers the car.

Steering wheel: turns the car

Hood: covers the engine

The pistons are connected to other engine parts. These parts make the wheels turn.

A driver pushes the pedals to make the car go and stop. A driver turns the steering wheel to steer the car.

**1886:** The Benz Patent-Motorwagen was invented. It was the first car to run on gas.

**1893:** The Duryea Motor Carriage was the first gas-powered car to be made in America.

**1908:** The Ford Model T was introduced. It was nicknamed the "Tin Lizzie."

**1913:** Ford began an assembly line for making cars.

**1913:** The Lincoln Highway became the first road to go across the United States.

**1924:** The car radio was introduced.

**1955:** The GM Sunmobile was the first solar car.

**1958:** The Saab GT750 was the first car to come with seat belts.

**1974:** The Oldsmobile Toronado was the first car to have airbags.

**1997:** The first Toyota Prius was sold in Japan. It was the first popular hybrid car.

## Cool Collectibles

Some people like to buy old cars. These are called classic cars. Some were built more than 100 years ago! They can look different from cars sold today.

Some classic car owners like to repair their old cars. They like to make their cars look like new again.

# Austin-Healey 3000

The Austin-Healey 3000 was a sports car made in the 1960s. It was made in England. Donald Healey designed the car. He was a race car driver. The Austin-Healey 3000 came in a hardtop or a removable top. It had a long hood.

**Years Made:**
1959 to 1967

**Maximum Horsepower (Hp):**
148 hp

**Top Speed:**
121 mph
(195 kmh)

## FUN FACT!

The Austin-Healey 3000's nickname is the "Big Healey." The car is small, but it has a big engine!

# Bugatti Type 57SC Atlantic

The Bugatti Type 57SC Atlantic is a rare car. Only four were made! The car has a long hood. It also has a ridge that runs down the middle. There are only two Bugatti Type 57SC Atlantics left in the world!

**Years Made:**
1936 to 1938

**Maximum Hp:**
220 hp

**Top Speed:**
123 mph
(198 kmh)

**Did You Know?**

The Woodie became popular with surfers. The car can hold many surfers—and lots of long surfboards!

# Chrysler Town & Country "Woodie"

This car is nicknamed the "Woodie." Why? It has wooden sides! Up to nine people can fit in a Woodie. This made it popular with families.

**Years Made:**
1947 to 1950;
1968 to 1969;
1983 to 1986

**Maximum Hp:**
135 hp
(1946 model)

**Top Speed:**
85 mph (137 kmh),
(1946 model)

# Ferrari 250 GTO

The 1962 Ferrari 250 GTO was built for racing. The inside of the car is not fancy. There isn't a heater. It is loud inside when being driven. The seats are not comfortable. But many people love the car.

*GTO* stands for "Gran Turismo Omologato." That means "grand tour approved" in Italian. GTO cars are race cars that can be bought and driven on the streets. They are not just for race car drivers.

**FUN FACT!**

Only 36 Ferrari 250 GTO cars were made.

### Did You Know?

The Ferrari logo is the Prancing Horse. It is a famous symbol of courage.

**Years Made:**
1962 to 1964

**Maximum Hp:**
300 hp

**Top Speed:**
174 mph
(280 kmh)

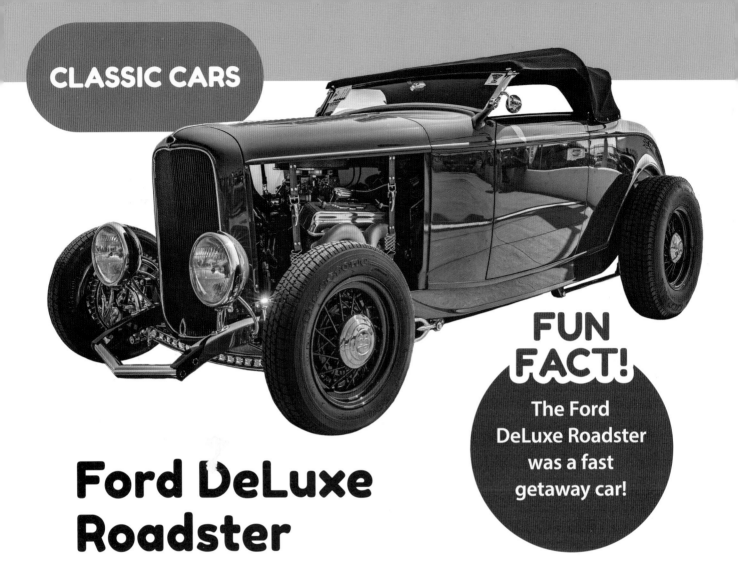

# Ford DeLuxe Roadster

**FUN FACT!**

The Ford DeLuxe Roadster was a fast getaway car!

The Ford DeLuxe Roadster was a fast car for the time. Both police officers and robbers liked to drive it! Robbers could speed away in this car, and police could chase them!

**Years Made:**
1932 to 1934

**Maximum Hp:**
85 hp

**Top Speed:**
65 mph
(105 kmh)

# Mercedes-Benz 300 SL "Gullwing"

The Mercedes-Benz 300 SL "Gullwing" has doors that swing upward. They look like a seagull's wings. That is how the Gullwing got its name.

**Years Made:**
1954 to 1957

**Maximum Hp:**
215 hp

**Top Speed:**
115 mph
(185 kmh)

# Rolls-Royce Silver Dawn Drophead

Rolls-Royce calls its convertible cars Dropheads. The top of the Silver Dawn Drophead folds down. The car also has curved fenders that go up and over its wheels.

What is missing from the Silver Dawn Drophead? Seat belts! Most older cars did not have seat belts. But this car had something that is in a lot of cars today: a start button. Instead of turning a key, drivers pushed a button to start the engine.

**Years Made:**
1949 to 1955

**Maximum Hp:**
128 hp

**Top Speed:**
87 mph
(140 kmh)

# FUN FACT!

The Rolls-Royce logo at the center of the wheel doesn't spin. It always stays upright.

# Shelby Cobra 427

The Shelby Cobra 427 is a famous sports car. It was designed by Carroll Shelby. Many Cobras have a racing stripe down the middle.

The Shelby Cobra 427 can go from 0 to 60 miles per hour (96.5 kmh) in under four seconds. That is fast!

There were fewer than 100 Shelby Cobra 427s made in all. But today, you can buy a kit to build your own!

## FUN FACT!

Carroll Shelby was a race car driver. He won his first race in 1952 and then won 12 more in 2 years.

**Years Made:**
1965 to 1967

**Maximum Hp:**
360 hp

**Top Speed:**
160 mph
(257 kmh)

## Did You Know?

Racing stripes helped people tell cars apart during a race. Now, racing stripes on cars are just for looks.

# Volkswagen Beetle

The Volkswagen Beetle was first built in Germany. It was made for people to drive around town and to work. The engine of this car is in the back. Most car engines are in the front.

This car was first named the Volkswagen Type 1. It looked like an insect, so people started calling it a beetle or a bug. The name Beetle eventually stuck.

## FUN FACT!

People in Bolivia call this car *peta*, which means "turtle."

**Years Made:**
1938 to 2003

**Maximum Hp:**
25 hp (1938 model)

**Top Speed:**
72 mph (116 kmh),
(1938 model)

## Did You Know?

The Volkswagen Beetle has been in lots of movies. It was the star in *Herbie* (1968) and *Herbie: Fully Loaded* (2005). Herbie the Beetle drives on its own.

## Getting around Town

Sedans are common cars. They usually seat four people. They have four doors and a closed roof. There is a separate area for a trunk. Coupes are similar to sedans. But they usually have two doors, not four. Coupes sit low to the ground.

# AUDI S5

The Audi S5 comes as a two-door or four-door car. The four-door version is called a Sportback. A Sportback is a blend of a sedan, coupe, and hatchback. There is also a version called the cabriolet. *Cabriolet* is another word for "convertible."

**Years Made:**
2007 to present

**Maximum Hp:**
349 hp

**Top Speed:**
155 mph (249 kmh)

## FUN FACT!

Audi was one of the first car companies to perform crash tests.

# BMW 3 Series

The BMW 3 Series cars have been around for a long time. They are still being made today. There have been seven generations of BMW 3 Series cars.

The first BMW 3 Series had something new: an angled dashboard. This made it easier for drivers to turn dials and push buttons for things such as the radio and heater.

**Years Made:**
1975 to present

**Maximum Hp:**
75 to 143 hp (first generation)

**Top Speed:**
99 mph (159 kmh), (first generation)

## FUN FACT!

The BMW 3 Series cars come in different styles.

## Did You Know?

In 1988, BMW built the first 3 Series car with all-wheel drive. This makes the car drive better on roads that are wet or icy.

# Honda Accord

The first Honda Accord was built in 1976. It was a hatchback. A hatchback is a car that has a hatch, or a door, that opens upward. The hatch covers the trunk area. Honda Accords are popular cars. They are good for families. They are also reliable. That means they run well and have few problems.

**Years Made:**
1976 to present

**Maximum Hp:**
192 hp (2023 model)

**Top Speed:**
116 mph (187 kmh),
(2023 model)

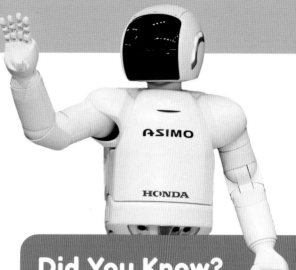

## Did You Know?

Honda began as a company that added engines to bikes. These became motorcycles. Honda still builds motorcycles. They also build jets, race cars, lawn mowers, and motors for boats and airplanes. They even build robots!

# Mini Cooper

Minis are famous for being small! Why are they so small? They were designed to be fuel-efficient. That means they would not use much gas. They also cost less than other cars. More people could afford them.

Minis drive well. They turn corners easily. They drive like go-karts. In 1962, John Cooper designed the Sport version of the Mini. John Cooper owned a car racing team.

**Years Made:**
1959 to present

**Maximum Hp:**
189 hp (2023 model)

**Top Speed:**
146 mph (235 kmh), (2023 model)

## FUN FACT!

A total of 29 people once fit in a Mini! This set a Guinness World Record.

## Did You Know?

Minis are very popular. They have been in movies. In 2003, a Mini was in the action movie *The Italian Job.*

# Toyota Camry

The Toyota Camry is one of the most popular cars in the world. There have been more than 10 million Camrys made at the Toyota factory in Kentucky. That's a lot of Camrys!

The Camry is fuel-efficient. It is also reliable. This sedan is good for families or for driving to work.

**FUN FACT!**

Toyota also builds boats!

**Years Made:**
1983 to present

**Maximum Hp:**
202 to 301 hp

**Top Speed:**
135 mph (217 kmh)

**Did You Know?**

The word *camry* is inspired by the Japanese word *kanmuri*. *Kanmuri* means "crown" in Japanese.

## Driving Ahead

Cars that run on gasoline make harmful gases. They can be bad for our planet. Carmakers wanted to build cars that are better for Earth. They looked for different ways to power cars.

Electric cars are powered by electricity. Hybrid cars use both gas and electricity. They use less gas than regular cars. Some cars run on hydrogen. Cars that run on hydrogen do not make harmful gases.

### FUN FACT!

Electric cars are sometimes called plug-ins. That's because they can be plugged in!

# Chevrolet Volt

The Chevrolet (or "Chevy") Volt is a plug-in hybrid. It runs mostly on electricity. It uses some gas too.

**Years Made:**
2011 to 2019

**Maximum Hp:**
149 hp (2019 model)

**Top Speed:**
98 mph (158 kmh)

# Fisker Karma

The Fisker Karma is a hybrid car. A hybrid car has a gas engine and an electric motor. The electric motor uses energy from batteries. The batteries are charged by the brakes and the gas engine.

## FUN FACT!

Drivers could add a solar panel to the Fisker Karma roof to further charge the car.

1890 Parker electric car

## Did You Know?

The first electric car was built in the United States in 1890. A lot of people became interested in electric cars. In 1908, the Model T was built. It ran on gas. More gas-powered cars were built. Electric cars didn't become popular again until the 2000s.

**Years Made:**
2012 to present

**Maximum Hp:**
402 hp

**Top Speed:**
125 mph (201 kmh)

# Rivian R1T

The Rivian R1T is a pickup truck powered by electricity. It was the first electric truck to be made. This truck is strong. It can tow up to 11,000 pounds (5,000 kg).

**Years Made:**
2021 to present

**Maximum Hp:**
600 to 835 hp
(2023 model)

**Top Speed:**
115 mph (185 kmh),
(2023 model)

## Did You Know?

This truck has a lot of cool features. It has a built-in flashlight and a "frunk." This is a trunk in the front.

# Tesla Model S Plaid

The Tesla Model S is an electric car. It is a sedan. It is good for families. The Tesla Model S can go fast. It can also go far before it needs to be charged.

The Tesla Model S Plaid is a superfast version of the Model S. It can go from 0 to 60 miles per hour (96.5 kmh) in 2.3 seconds.

**Years Made:**
2021 to present

**Maximum Hp:**
1021 hp

**Top Speed:**
175 mph (282 kmh)

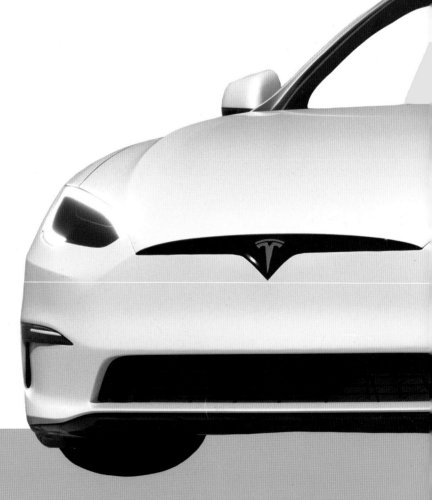

## Did You Know?

Horsepower is a way to talk about the power of an engine. A long time ago, horses were used to pull things. People compared engines to horses. A car with high horsepower is powerful.

## FUN FACT!

The Tesla Model S Plaid can go almost as fast as a NASCAR race car!

# Toyota Mirai

The Toyota Mirai is the first hydrogen-powered car that people can buy. There is no middle seat in the back row of this car. Taking it out made the car drive better.

**Years Made:**
2016 to present

**Maximum Hp:**
182 hp
(2023 model)

**Top Speed:**
106 mph (171 kmh)

# Toyota Prius

The Toyota Prius was the first popular hybrid car. This hybrid car can be plugged in at home. This makes it easy to charge.

More than 5 million Prius cars have been made. They are still being made and sold today.

**Years Made:**
2000 to present

**Maximum Hp:**
196 hp (2023 model)

**Top Speed:**
115 mph (185 kmh), (2023 model)

# Family Vehicles

Minivans and station wagons are larger cars. They can carry more people and belongings. They are popular with families.

Some kids play sports. They need room for sports gear. Some kids play a musical instrument. They need room for their instruments. Babies and small kids need to sit in car seats. Car seats take up room too.

**FUN FACT!**

The Dodge Caravan started a craze for minivans.

# Dodge Caravan

The Dodge Caravan was the first minivan to be sold. It can seat up to seven people. More than 200,000 were sold in the first year. A new version was built the next year. It could carry cargo. It was called the Mini Ram Van.

**Years Made:**
1984 to 2020

**Maximum Hp:**
283 hp (2020 model)

**Top Speed:**
140 mph (225 kmh), (2020 model)

# Honda Odyssey

The Honda Odyssey is a minivan. Designers worked on it in secret. They told everyone they were working on a private jet. The Odyssey first had doors that swung open like a regular car. Later, it had sliding doors.

Newer Odyssey vans have a camera so drivers can watch the passengers in the second and third rows of seats.

## Did You Know?

Many people think the 1923 Star Station Wagon was the first station wagon. These cars were used to take people to and from train stations. That's how they got their name!

# FUN FACT!

*Odyssey* is another word for "journey."

**Years Made:**
1995 to present

**Maximum Hp:**
280 hp (2023 model)

**Top Speed:**
111 mph (179 kmh), (2023 model)

47

# Stout Scarab

The Stout Scarab was a different kind of car. In 1936, it looked like something from the future. It is silver and shiny.

Some people call this the world's first minivan. It is long and carries lots of people. Its seats can be moved around. Some seats can swivel, or turn. Only the driver's seat cannot be moved.

**Year Made:**
1936

**Maximum Hp:**
85 hp

**Top Speed:**
80 mph (129 kmh)

# FUN FACT!

The Scarab is an expensive car. Only nine were built!

# Subaru Outback

The Subaru Outback is a crossover car. It is part station wagon and part sport utility vehicle. It was the first crossover.

The Outback drives like a car but it also has all-wheel drive. This makes it good for driving on dirt roads or in winter weather. It is a car made for adventure.

Australian Outback

## FUN FACT!
The Subaru Outback was named after the desert area in Australia.

**Years Made:**
1994 to present

**Maximum Hp:**
182 to 260 hp (2023 model)

**Top Speed:**
120 mph (193 kmh)

## Power under the Hood

Muscle cars are powerful. They can drive fast. Muscle cars are usually bigger than sports cars. Muscle cars often have a boxlike shape. They became popular in the 1960s. They are still popular today.

**FUN FACT!**

Muscle cars are super strong. That's how they got their name!

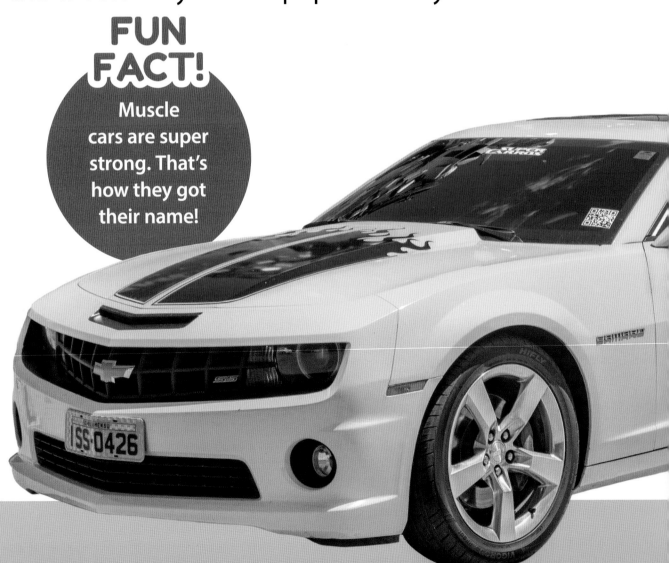

# Chevrolet Camaro

The Chevy Camaro was a hit from the start. There were 220,000 Camaros sold in the first year alone! The Camaro was first named the Chevrolet Panther. Chevy changed it to Camaro instead. The name Camaro was inspired by the word *comrade*, which means "friend."

**Years Made:**
1966 to present

**Maximum Hp:**
275 to 650 hp
(2023 model)

**Top Speed:**
198 mph (319 kmh),
(2023 model)

**Did You Know?**

A 2007 Chevy Camaro was in the movie *Transformers*. The car plays the character Bumblebee in the movie.

# Chevrolet Impala SS

The Chevrolet Impala SS was a popular muscle car. The Impala of the 1960s had a powerful engine. It was called the 409. The Beach Boys band celebrated it in their song "409."

**Years Made:**
1961 to 1969;
1994 to 1996

**Maximum Hp:**
260 hp

**Top Speed:**
145 mph (233 kmh),
(1996 model)

# Dodge Challenger SRT Demon

The Dodge Challenger SRT Demon is fast. It can travel a quarter mile (0.4 km) in less than 10 seconds. The car doesn't have any back seats. The passenger seat can be removed too. This helps the car go even faster.

**Years Made:**
2018 to present

**Maximum Hp:**
840 hp

**Top Speed:**
211 mph (340 kmh)

# Dodge Charger

The Dodge Charger is a popular muscle car. It has a bigger trunk than other muscle cars. There is more room to store things.

**FUN FACT!**

Today, the 2023 Dodge Charger is the world's fastest four-door muscle car!

## Did You Know?

In 2001, the 1970 Dodge Charger R/T was in the movie *The Fast and the Furious.* The car became famous again after the movie. It even got its own Lego set!

**Years Made:**
1966 to present

**Maximum Hp:**
292 to 797 hp
(2023 model)

**Top Speed:**
203 mph (327 kmh),
(2023 model)

A 1969 Dodge Charger was in the TV show *The Dukes of Hazzard.* It was called the "General Lee." The show made the Charger popular. It was hard to find one to buy.

# Ford Mustang

The Ford Mustang is a famous muscle car. It first came out in 1964. Ford planned on selling 100,000 that year. But the car became popular. On the first day alone, 22,000 Mustangs were sold! By 1966, Ford had built 1 million Mustangs.

**Years Made:**
1964 to present

**Maximum Hp:**
271 hp (1964 model)

**Top Speed:**
128 mph (206 kmh), (1964 model)

### Did You Know?

The Ford Mustang was the first muscle car to be called a pony car. That's because a mustang is a type of horse: a fast horse!

## FUN FACT!

An electric version of the car came out in 2020. It is called the Mustang Mach-E.

# Plymouth Road Runner

The Plymouth Road Runner was named after a cartoon character. Road Runner is a bird from the *Looney Tunes* TV series. The bird is famous for moving fast. It also says "beep, beep." The Plymouth Road Runner has a horn that goes "beep, beep," just like the character.

## Did You Know?

The Plymouth Road Runner has a simple interior. This made it less expensive than other similar cars.

**Years Made:**
1968 to 1980

**Maximum Hp:**
120 hp (1980 model)

**Top Speed:**
121 mph (195 kmh)

## FUN FACT!

Plymouth paid the company that owned *Looney Tunes* $50,000 to be able to use the name Road Runner.

# Pontiac Firebird Trans Am

The Pontiac Firebird Trans Am had a powerful engine. The 1978 model could go from 0 to 60 miles per hour (9.5 kmh) in 7.6 seconds. The car has a firebird logo on the hood. It is nicknamed the screaming chicken.

**Years Made:**
1970 to 1981

**Maximum Hp:**
220 hp

**Top Speed:**
130 mph (209 kmh)

## Did You Know?

The Pontiac Firebird Trans Am was in the movie *Smokey and the Bandit*. Actor Burt Reynolds drove the 1976 model. The movie made the car even more popular and boosted sales.

## AMC AMX

The AMC AMX was sold in the 1960s. This muscle car only had two seats. This was unusual for muscle cars.

## Buick Grand National

This car was first made in 1982. The 1987 Grand National was sold with a matching jacket.

# Chevrolet Chevelle SS

The 1970 Chevelle SS was called the "King of the Muscle Cars." At the time, it was the muscle car with the most powerful engine.

# Pontiac GTO

This was the first car to be called a muscle car. It was named after a famous Ferrari race car.

## Keep on Truckin'

Pickup trucks are popular. They have a cab at the front. This is where people sit. The back of the truck has a flat, open area. This is called the truck bed. It is a place to store things. Pickup trucks help people move large items. They can be handy!

# Chevrolet Silverado

Pickup trucks, like the Chevy Silverado, can do a lot of different tasks. They can tow things such as boats and trailers.

**Years Made:**
1999 to present

**Maximum Hp:**
277 to 420 hp

**Top Speed:**
112 mph
(180 kmh)

## Did You Know?

Before 1955, pickups were used mostly as work vehicles. In 1955, Chevy made the Chevy Task Force. This truck was more comfortable inside. It was more like a regular car. The work truck was changing. It was becoming a truck anyone could enjoy!

# Ford F-Series

The F-Series is a group of pickup trucks made by Ford. The F-Series has been popular. They have been the best-selling trucks in the United States since 1982.

One of the trucks is called the Raptor. It has a lot of cool features. It has a big engine and special tires. It can be driven off-road.

# FUN FACT!

The Raptor's tailgate has a ruler on it. Construction workers can measure items right on the truck!

**Years Made:**
1948 to present

**Maximum Hp:**
450 to 700 hp
(Ford F-150 Raptor)

**Top Speed:**
120 mph (193 kmh),
(Ford F-150 Raptor)

# Ford Ranger

The first Ford with the name Ranger was a sedan. It was not a truck. The Ford Ranger pickup truck was first sold in 1983. It is a smaller pickup truck.

Today, the Ford Ranger comes with two types of cabs. The SuperCab and the SuperCrew can fit up to six people.

**Years Made:**
1983 to 2012;
2019 to present

**Maximum Hp:**
270 hp (2023 model)

**Top Speed:**
128 mph (206 kmh),
(2023 model)

# GMC Syclone

The GMC Syclone was a street-only truck. That meant it wasn't to be driven off-road. There was a warning on the Syclone. It said the truck could be damaged if taken off-road. The GMC Syclone was rare. Fewer than 3,000 were made.

**Years Made:**
1991 to 1993

**Maximum Hp:**
280 hp

**Top Speed:**
124 mph (200 kmh)

**FUN FACT!**

The Syclone was the fastest pickup truck of its time.

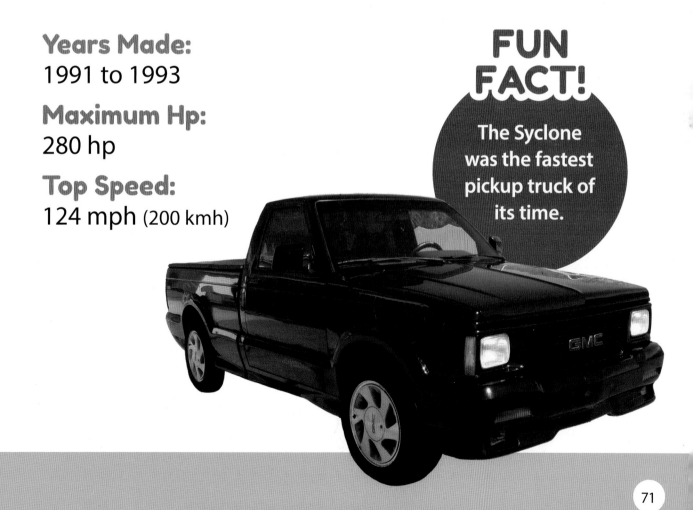

# Jeep Gladiator

The Gladiator is a type of truck made by Jeep. In 1987, Jeep stopped making these trucks. In 2020, Jeep started making them again.

**Years Made:**
1963 to 1987;
2020 to present

**Maximum Hp:**
260 to 285 hp

**Top Speed:**
130 mph (209 kmh)

# Toyota Hilux

The Toyota Hilux is one of the most popular trucks in the world. But the Hilux is not sold in the United States. Why not? It is not built there. To sell it in the United States, Toyota would have to pay a tax. This would make the truck too expensive for customers.

**Years Made:**
1968 to present

**Maximum Hp:**
201 hp

**Top Speed:**
121 mph (195 kmh)

## GMC Sierra

The 2024 Sierra EV Denali is GMC's most powerful truck. It can pull up to 9,500 pounds (4,309 kg)! That's about the weight of an ambulance.

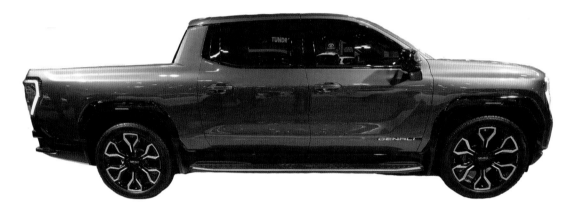

## Ram

A ram hood ornament is on the front of the Ram. These pickups have been named Truck of the Year five times.

# Toyota Tacoma

*Tacoma* is the Salish word for Mount Rainier. Mount Rainier is a tall mountain near Seattle, Washington. The name represents toughness.

# Toyota Tundra

The Toyota Tundra is built and sold only in North America.

## Start Your Engines!

Race cars are special. It's amazing to see cars go so fast! There are many types of car races. Some are on regular streets. Others are off-road. Some races are on special racetracks. There are different cars for different types of races.

# Audi Quattro S1 E2

The Audi Quattro S1 E2 is a famous rally car.

**Years Made:**
1985 to 1986

**Maximum Hp:**
592 hp

**Top Speed:**
136 mph (219 kmh)

## Did You Know?

Rally racing takes place on streets or dirt roads. The drivers race against the clock. Co-drivers ride in the car. They coach the drivers.

# Audi R8 LMP

The 24 Hours of Le Mans is a famous car race. It happens in France every year. The idea is simple. Cars drive on a racetrack for 24 hours. The car that goes the farthest is the winner.

The Audi R8 LMP is one of the best race cars of all time. The Audi R8 LMP has won the 24 Hours of Le Mans five times in six years.

**Years Made:**
 2000 to 2006

**Maximum Hp:**
520 to 625 hp

**Top Speed:**
210 mph (338 kmh)

# Chevrolet Nova

The 1977 Chevy Nova was a famous race car. It was the car driven by Dale Earnhardt. He was a famous NASCAR race car driver. The car was painted silver and black.

**FUN FACT!**

A stock car is a regular car that has been fixed up for racing.

Dale Earnhardt

## Did You Know?

NASCAR holds stock car races. There are different NASCAR races. The Daytona 500 is a famous race. Drivers race for 500 miles (804.7 km) around a track. It takes 200 laps to reach 500 miles.

**Years Made:**
1962 to 1988

**Maximum Hp:**
700 hp

**Top Speed:**
106 mph (171 kmh)

# Dodge Charger Daytona

**Years Made:**
1969 to 1970;
2006 to 2009;
2013;
2017 to present

**Maximum Hp:**
425 hp

**Top Speed:**
200 mph (322 kmh)

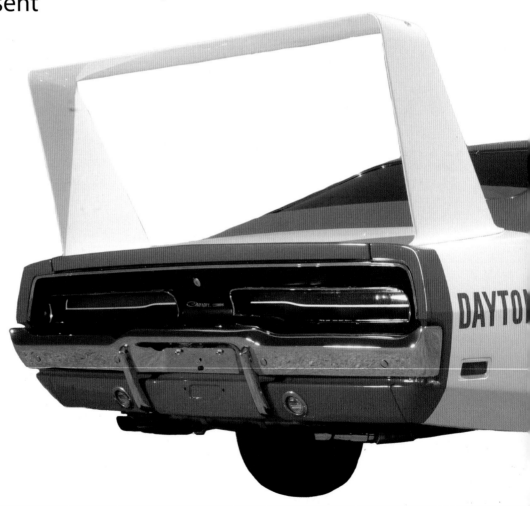

The 1969 Dodge Charger Daytona was a good race car. It was the first NASCAR car to reach 200 miles per hour (322 kmh) on the race track.

The car was too powerful though. NASCAR didn't think it was designed in a fair way. The car wasn't allowed to race anymore. NASCAR made new rules that controlled the design of race cars. The races became fairer. The rules also made the cars safer.

**FUN FACT!**

Many people thought the 1969 Dodge Charger Daytona was ugly.

# Ferrari 125 F1

Formula 1 cars are a famous type of race car. Ferrari's first Formula 1 car was the Ferrari 125 F1. It first raced at the Italian Grand Prix in 1948. It came in third place.

**Years Made:**
1947 to 1950

**Maximum Hp:**
280 hp

**Top Speed:**
131 mph (211 kmh)

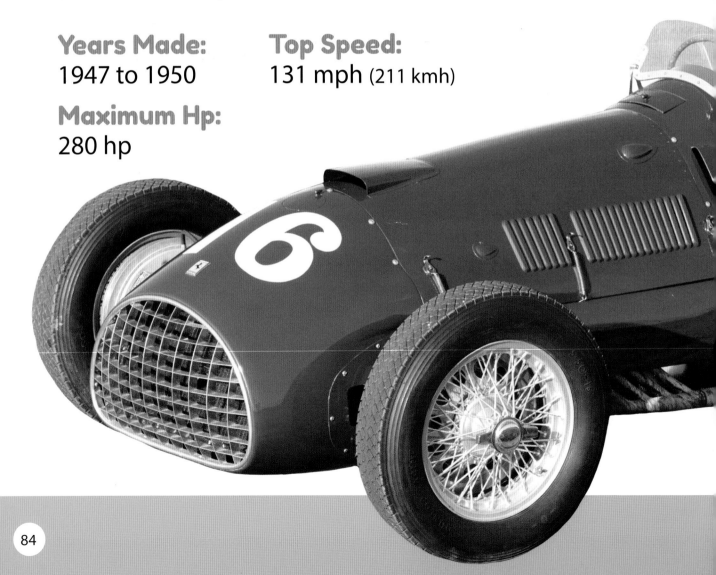

## Did You Know?

Formula 1 is a series of car races that happen all over the world. The cars race on a track. Each car has a team. The teams are made up of drivers, mechanics, engineers, and more.

# Ford GT40

The Ford GT40 is a famous race car from the 1960s. Ford and Ferrari are carmakers. Ford wanted to beat Ferrari in car races. So, Ford built the GT40.

## FUN FACT!

*GT* stands for "grand touring."

The car didn't start out winning races. In 1964, three Ford GT40 cars crashed and caught fire at the 24 Hours of Le Mans race. But Ford didn't give up. Starting in 1966, the Ford GT40 won the Le Mans race four years in a row!

**Years Made:**
1964 to 1969

**Maximum Hp:**
484 hp

**Top Speed:**
210 mph (338 kmh)

# Hudson Hornet

The Hudson Hornet was a NASCAR race car from the 1950s. The car won 79 races between 1951 and 1955. That helped carmakers sell more cars.

The Hudson carmakers had a famous saying: "Win on Sunday, sell on Monday." One of the first female car designers helped make the Hudson Hornet.

**Years Made:**
1951 to 1957

**Maximum Hp:**
145 hp

**Top Speed:**
121 mph (195 kmh)

## Did You Know?

The Hudson Hornet was the inspiration behind the Doc Hudson character in the movie *Cars*.

# Lotus 72

The Lotus 72 is thought to be one of the best F1 cars ever. It was aerodynamic. The car was also lightweight. It was shaped like a wedge, or a piece of pie. This was unusual for race cars at the time.

**FUN FACT!**

The Lotus 72 competed in 90 Formula 1 races.

**Years Made:**
1970 to 1975

**Maximum Hp:**
440 to 475 hp

**Top Speed:**
200 mph (322 kmh)

### Did You Know?
The Lotus Espirit S1 was in the 1977 James Bond movie *The Spy Who Loved Me*. In the movie, the car turns into a submarine.

# McLaren F1 GTR

The McLaren F1 GTR raced in F1 races. It also raced in the 24 Hours of Le Mans. There were 100 McLaren F1 cars built. Only 28 were made for racing. Some of the cars were longer than others. They were called longtails.

**Years Made:**
1995 to 1997

**Maximum Hp:**
600 hp

**Top Speed:**
240 mph (386 kmh)

# Mercedes-AMG F1 W11 EQ Performance

Some people think the Mercedes W11 is the fastest Formula 1 car ever. In 2020, the car set a record for the fastest average lap at an F1 race. It could do a lap in about 1 minute and 18 seconds.

**Year Made:**
2020

**Maximum Hp:**
1,025 hp

**Top Speed:**
164 mph
(264 kmh)

# Ford Mustang Boss 429

The 1969 Ford Mustang Boss 429 was a muscle car. It had a NASCAR-style engine. Fewer than 1,500 Mustang Boss 429s were made. The Boss 429 was designed to race in NASCAR. It never did.

Until the 1980s, NASCAR had a rule. In order to race, a car had to be available to the public to buy. Ford would have to make at least 500 Boss 429s each year. The company didn't want to spend the money. So, Ford took the engine out of the 429 and placed it in another car to race.

## Did You Know?

The Boss 429 is one of the most valuable Mustangs.

# Ford Thunderbird

In 1987, race car driver Bill Elliott set a NASCAR speed record. He drove a Ford Thunderbird. The car raced at 212.809 miles per hour (342.5 kmh). This is still NASCAR's fastest lap ever.

**FUN FACT!**

The Ford Thunderbird was also known as the T-Bird.

## A Need for Speed

Sports cars are popular with people who want to drive fast. Most sports cars are small. They are often built low to the ground. They have powerful engines.

Usually, sports cars only have two seats. Sports cars have good handling. This means they can turn and be steered easily.

# Chevrolet Corvette

The 1953 Corvette only came in one color. It was white with a red interior.

There is a type of Corvette called the Stingray. Its nickname is the "Road Shark."

The Corvette is still one of the most popular sports cars in America.

**Years Made:**
1953 to present

**Maximum Hp:**
670 hp

**Top Speed:**
189 mph (304 kmh), (2023 model)

**FUN FACT!**

The Corvette was named after a small warship.

# DeLorean DMC-12

The DeLorean DMC-12 was in the *Back to the Future* movies. In the movies, it travels through time. It also goes from 0 to 88 miles per hour (141.6 kmh) in a few seconds. In real life, the car doesn't go that fast. It also doesn't time travel!

**Years Made:**
1981 to 1983

**Maximum Hp:**
130 hp

**Top Speed:**
130 mph
(209 kmh)

**FUN FACT!**

The doors of the DeLorean make the car look like it has wings!

# Dodge Viper

The engineers at Lamborghini helped to design the engine for the Dodge Viper. The Dodge Viper's engine is similar to a Lamborghini's. It is powerful. Venom Red was the most popular Dodge Viper color.

**Years Made:**
1991 to 2017

**Maximum Hp:**
645 hp
(2017 model)

**Top Speed:**
206 mph (332 kmh),
(2017 model)

# Ferrari Enzo

The Ferrari Enzo was named after the creator of the company Ferrari. His first name was Enzo. He is one of the most famous carmakers of all time.

The Ferrari Enzo is the most expensive Ferrari ever made. It costs more than half a million dollars!

# FUN FACT!

There were fewer than 400 Ferrari Enzos made.

**Years Made:**
2002 to 2005

**Maximum Hp:**
660 hp

**Top Speed:**
217 mph (349 kmh)

# Koenigsegg Jesko Absolut

**Years Made:**
2021 to present

**Maximum Hp:**
1,600 hp

**Top Speed:**
300 mph (483 kmh)

The Koenigsegg Jesko Absolut is made in Sweden. It was made by Christian von Koenigsegg. Christian named the car after his father, Jesko.

**FUN FACT!**
The name *Absolut* means this is the *absolute* fastest Jesko car the company will make.

# Lamborghini Aventador SVJ Roadster

**Years Made:**
2019 to present

**Maximum Hp:**
770 hp

**Top Speed:**
218 mph (351 kmh)

The Lamborghini Aventador SVJ Roadster is expensive. Only 800 of these cars have been made. They have all been sold!

*Roadster* means that the car is a convertible. The roof of the car can be put in the frunk.

# McLaren Senna

The McLaren Senna is built for normal streets. But it is built to drive like a race car. The McLaren Senna costs 1 million dollars. The Senna is named after Brazilian Formula 1 driver Ayrton Senna.

**Years Made:**
2018 to present

**Maximum Hp:**
789 hp

**Top Speed:**
208 mph (335 kmh)

## FUN FACT!

Buyers can choose to have the car painted any color.

# Pagani Huayra Roadster

Each Pagani Huarya Roadster cost more than 3 million dollars. There were only 100 cars made. All 100 sold quickly—even with such a huge price tag!

Pagani custom built each car. That means the buyers could choose special details.

**Year Made:**
2017

**Maximum Hp:**
791 hp

**Top Speed:**
238 mph (383 kmh)

The Spyder has a removable roof that can be stored in its frunk.

# Porsche 918 Spyder

Many people think of the Porsche 918 Spyder as the first hybrid hyper car. It is fast and drives well. Like most hyper cars, the Spyder was rare. Only 918 cars of this model were made.

**Years Made:**
2013 to 2015

**Top Speed:**
214 mph (344 kmh)

**Maximum Hp:**
608 hp

# Toyota Supra

The Toyota Supra Mark IV is a famous sports car. The Supra was in the movie *The Fast and the Furious.*

**Years Made:**
1978 to 2002;
2019 to present

**Maximum Hp:**
320 hp

**Top Speed:**
155 mph (249 kmh)

## Did You Know?

The 1994 Supra had problems. It was unsafe and unreliable. It was banned by the National Highway Traffic Safety Administration.

## Acura NSX

The interior of this car was inspired by the cockpit of an F-16 fighter jet. The Acura NSX has a glass rooftop like the F-16. The driver can see all around. This helps the driver maneuver the car.

## Ferrari F40

The first F40s had a very thin layer of paint to make the car lighter, which helped it go fast.

# Lamborghini Countach

This car did not have a bumper originally. To be able to drive this car in America, the makers had to add a bumper.

# Mazda MX-5 Miata

The MX-5 Miata has an electric roof. It takes 12 seconds to lower the top.

*SUV* stands for "sport utility vehicle." These cars are larger than sedans. They sit higher off the ground. Many families like SUVs. They can carry a lot of people and things.

SUVs often have four-wheel drive. That means the engine powers all four wheels. This helps cars drive safely off-road and in the snow.

# Ford Bronco

The 1965 Bronco had the nickname "GOAT." That nickname stands for "goes over any terrain."

**Years Made:**
1965 to 1996;
2021 to present

**Maximum Hp:**
105 hp

**Top Speed:**
80 mph (129 kmh)

# Ford Explorer

The Ford Explorer is popular in the United States. It is the best-selling SUV of all time.

**Years Made:**
1991 to present

**Top Speed:**
146 mph (235 kmh)

**Maximum Hp:**
300 to 400 hp

# GMC Hummer

The Hummer is a famous car that got a bad reputation. It was heavy and used a lot of gas. It was thought to be bad for the environment.

The makers stopped building the Hummer in 2010. They brought it back in 2022.

**Years Made:**
1992 to 2010 (gas-powered);
2022 to present
(electric-powered)

**Maximum Hp:**
1,000 hp (2023 EV version)

**Top Speed:**
106 mph (171 kmh)

# International Harvester Scout

Many people think the International Harvester Scout was one of the first SUVs. The company who built the car also made tractors. The Scout had four-wheel drive. Families could take it off-road for camping.

**Years Made:**
1961 to 1980

**Maximum Hp:**
93 hp (1961 model)

**Top Speed:**
76 mph (122 kmh)

# Jeep Cherokee

The 1984 Jeep Cherokee was small compared to other SUVs. It could still tow things such as trailers and boats. Jeep nicknamed it the "Sportswagon." The 1984 Jeep Cherokee made SUVs popular.

**Years Made:**
1984 to present

**Maximum Hp:**
110 hp

**Top Speed:**
94 mph (151 kmh)

# Jeep Wrangler

Jeeps started as vehicles made for the US Army during World War II. They can go over dirt and rocks easily. They were used to carry troops and deliver supplies. The first Jeep was called a Willys Quad.

## Did You Know?

Jeeps were once used as Zamboni machines on ice rinks. Zambonis help to smooth out ice before hockey games.

**Years Made:**
1986 to present

**Maximum Hp:**
285 hp (2023 model)

**Top Speed:**
122 mph (196 kmh), (2023 model)

# Land Rover Defender

The first Land Rover Defender was unusual. It had a steering wheel in the center of the car. It fit 12 people inside. This made it a bus! The Land Rover 110 was built in 1983. In 1990, the name was changed to Defender.

**Years Made:**
1990 to 2016;
2020 to present

**Maximum Hp:**
518 hp (2023 model)

**Top Speed:**
149 mph (240 kmh),
(2023 model)

# Toyota Land Cruiser FJ40

The Toyota Land Cruiser FJ40 is popular around the world. In 2019, it was sold in 170 countries. By then, 10 million Land Cruisers had been sold!

**Years Made:**
1960 to 2022

**Maximum Hp:**
305 to 409 hp
(2022 model)

**Top Speed:**
130 mph
(209 kmh),
(2022 model)

# Cadillac Escalade

The Escalade is a luxurious, or fancy, SUV. It was built to compete with the Lincoln Navigator. The Escalade is one of only three Cadillac vehicles that are made outside of the United States.

# Chevrolet Suburban

The Chevy Suburban has been around since 1935. There have been many generations, but the Suburban has been around longer than any other car still being made.

# Honda CR-V

*CR-V* stands for "comfortable runabout vehicle." Its design was based on the Honda Civic.

# Land Rover Range Rover

Range Rovers have been used by militaries all around the world. But they were also driven by the Queen of England. In 1971, the Range Rover was on display in the famous French museum the Louvre for its design.

# What's Down the Road?

The future of cars is exciting. Carmakers have a lot of ideas. Many cars will be better for the environment. Some cars may help rescue people after disasters such as earthquakes. There may even be flying cars!

# Audi AI:TRAIL

The AI:TRAIL is not for sale yet. It will be great for people who like to drive off-road. The cabin will be made entirely of glass. People will be able to see all around them.

# DS X E-Tense

The DS X E-Tense will be autonomous. On one side, the driver will control the car. On the other side, the car will take over. The driver will be able to sit back and relax!

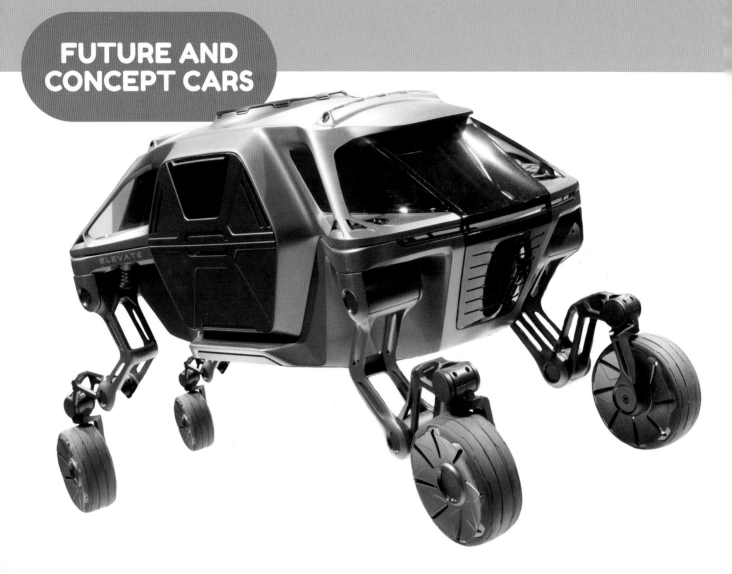

# Hyundai Elevate

Sometimes it is hard for ambulances to reach people in emergencies. The Hyundai Elevate will help. It will be on giant legs. The car will be able to "walk" into disaster zones.

# KleinVision AirCar

Believe it or not, there is already a flying car! The AirCar can turn into an aircraft in about three minutes.

# Tesla Cybertruck

The Tesla Cybertruck is a concept electric truck. It is super strong and can tow heavy things. It can also hold a lot of cargo in the truck bed. But it will feel different from a truck while driving. It is designed to drive like a sports car.

## Did You Know?

The Cybertruck can drive 500 miles (804.7 km) on one charge.

## FUN FACT!

The Tesla Cybertruck can drive itself!

# GLOSSARY

**aerodynamic**
Designed for air to travel over it to maximize speed.

**all-wheel drive**
When a car's engine powers all four wheels, not just two.

**autonomous**
Describing a car that can drive without a human.

**buggy**
A small carriage to transport people, typically pulled by a horse.

**cargo**
Items stored in a car.

**generation**
A new version of the same car model.

**hydrogen**
A substance that is colorless, odorless, and flammable (can catch on fire easily).

**hyper car**
A high-performance sports car.

**maneuver**
To move skillfully or carefully

**off-road**
When a car is built to be used on rough, uneven land such as dirt roads.

**Salish**
A group of Native Americans from the northwestern United States and British Columbia.

**solar**
Having to do with energy from the sun's light.

# TO LEARN MORE

## More Books to Read

Andrus, Aubre. *National Geographic Readers: Let's Go!* National Geographic Kids, 2019.

Bécue, Benjamin; Mercier, Julie; Turdera, Cristian. *Do You Know?: Vehicles and Transportation.* Twirl, 2021.

Bova, Dan. *Road & Track Crew's Big & Fast Cars: 701 Totally Amazing Facts!* Hearst Home Kids, 2022.

## Online Resources

To learn more about cars, please visit **abdobooklinks.com** or scan this QR code. These links are routinely monitored and updated to provide the most current information available.

## INDEX

# PHOTO CREDITS